# 20th Century
# Bathroom Design

by
# Kohler®

Tina Skinner

Schiffer Publishing Ltd®

4880 Lower Valley Road, Atglen, PA 19310 USA

## Dedication

To my mother, whose bathrooms change face constantly, but whose heart never wavers.

Skinner, Tina.
    20th century bathroom design by kohler / Tina Skinner.
        p.   cm.
    ISBN 0-7643-0614-6 (softcover)
    1. Plumbing fixtures--United States--History--20th century. 2. Kohler Company. 3. Bathrooms--United States--Design and construction--History--20th century. 4. Interior decoration--United States--History--20th century. I. Title.
TH6488.S55    1998
747.7'8--dc21                                    98-22761
                                                    CIP

Book design by Blair Loughrey
Typeset in Bernhard Mod BT/Times New Roman

ISBN: 0-7643-0614-6
Printed in China

Published by Schiffer Publishing Ltd.
4880 Lower Valley Road
Atglen, PA 19310
Phone: (610) 593-1777; Fax: (610) 593-2002
E-mail: Schifferbk@aol.com
Please write for a free catalog.
This book may be purchased from the publisher.
Please include $3.95 for shipping.

In Europe Schiffer books are distributed by
Bushwood Books
6 Marksbury Avenue
Kew Gardens
Surrey TW9 4JF England
Phone: 44 (0) 181 392-8585; Fax: 44 (0) 181 392-9876
E-mail: Bushwd@aol.com

Please try your bookstore first.

We are interested in hearing from authors with book ideas on related subjects.

# Table of Contents

# Acknowledgments

Special thanks to Cheryl Prepster of Kohler Co., who found time to help me compile all this material between phone calls from all those curious homeowners trying to identify their old bathtubs and sinks. And thanks to Peter Fetterer, her boss, who let her take the time to help me. Most importantly, however, thanks to an enormous company that isn't too big to make a quick decision without a million committee meetings.

# Introduction

Growing up, the greatest luxury I could imagine was a big, enameled cast-iron tub. Not for the bathroom, however. As a little girl, these tubs were valuable in my mind because my mind was obsessed with horses. Such tubs were ideal water troughs.

Ironically, that's how the Kohler Co. got its start in the plumbing business, way back in 1883, when John Michael Kohler enameled a cast-iron horse trough/hog scalder and advertised that it would also serve as a bathtub. From a farm implements company founded in 1873, a plumbing dynasty was born. Today, those old cast-iron tubs and sinks are valuable, not in the barnyard, but in a restored state as household treasures.

That's because they were built to last. By 1911, Kohler was leading the way in plumbing fixture innovations. Formerly bathtubs were made from two pieces of cast iron welded together, the company invented a one-piece tub that was more aesthetic and sanitary. By 1926, it was making brass faucets, traps, and drains with chromium and gold finishes that added to the luxury, and it added vitreous china sinks and toilets to its line the following year. That year, 1927, was a big one for the company. That's when Kohler perfected color matching technology, enabling it to match cast-iron enamel to china glazes and offer bathroom sets—tub, toilet, and lavatory—in matching Spring Green, Lavender, Autumn Brown, Old Ivory, and Horizon Blue, along with white.

Kohler continued to set standards in bathroom luxury for the next three decades, but the company really soared to the lead in the mid-1960s with "The Bold Look of Kohler" advertising campaign. Combined with a relentless onslaught of new products and color introductions, Kohler's advertising blitz propelled it to the top spot in the plumbing business by the end of the 1970s.

Making it to the top hasn't slowed Kohler's climb, however. Still family owned and operated, Kohler continues to stress innovation. The most obvious display of this is the Kohler Design Center in Kohler, Wisconsin, where consultants and designers work on product development and use, and provide guidance to homeowners and builders with new home and remodeling projects. The center includes a Product Pavilion, where Kohler Co. products are displayed; the Water Deck, where water cascades from faucets and swirls in fourteen whirlpool baths; the Designer Room Gallery, where nationally recognized designers show off bathroom and kitchen designs ranging from traditional to avant-garde, and a museum, where the history of Kohler Co. is traced. Short of going there yourself, this book is the best guide to the Kohler Co.'s contribution to the American bathroom.

# The Advent of Color

Kohler started off the century with an advertising campaign designed to reach right to the heart of every family—through the children. The company commissioned artists to create Rockwell-like drawings of children in the bathroom, helping mommy by the kitchen sink, or playing by the Kohler generator, and plastered national magazines like *The Saturday Evening Post, Liberty, Literary Digest*, and *House and Garden* with these images. The ads ran with messages about the importance of early lessons in cleanliness and the pride in home associated with fine plumbing. Kohler also started promoting a message that would form the crux of its ad campaign over the next four decades—the need for additional bathrooms in order to create family harmony. In 1927, Kohler established itself as a leader in bathroom design, being one of the first companies to perfect color matching between vitreous china glazes and cast-iron enamels. Now sinks, toilets, and bathtubs all could match, in a choice of six colors offered by Kohler of Kohler.

Plumbing was pretty basic as the century got underway. Here a 1923 brochure shows what, in that day and age, was a luxury bathroom, featuring a built-in bathtub, "elaborate shower fixtures," a lavatory or sink with hot and cold water taps, and a "closet combination" toilet. At this time, the company made the claim that "Kohler Ware is universally known for its uniformly clear white enamel."

As early as 1915, Kohler was working to transform the bath into a fun place. In this *Saturday Evening Post* ad, the company boasts about its "easy-to-clean enamel." Also, the ad points out that the company name is stamped in faint blue on every Kohler product.

"Colonna" Bath,
Plate No. K-64

This trade-mark appears on every piece of KOHLER enameled plumbing ware. It is incorporated in faint blue in the enamel, at the points indicated by the arrows, and corresponds in size to the name "KOHLER" shown in the illustration.

"Bretton" Lavatory,
Plate No. K-580

In this 1922 *Saturday Evening Post* ad, Kohler reflects the theme it has carried through the years, attempting to link social status to the water closet: "The furnishings in the rest of your home reflect, from necessity, the limitations of your income. But whether this one room in question reflects your sense of refinement, your ideals of hygiene and sanitation, is a matter, not of money, but of pride."

The walls in Kohler's corporate offices in Wisconsin are a showcase for artwork commissioned over the years for advertising campaigns. This 1924 advertisement was one of the first in an extensive Kohler campaign run in national magazines. These ads featured oil paintings commissioned by Kohler that showed its products in use by rosy cheeked children. "The beautiful tub pictured above can be yours for a very reasonable investment, with magnificent returns in comfort, convenience, and pride."

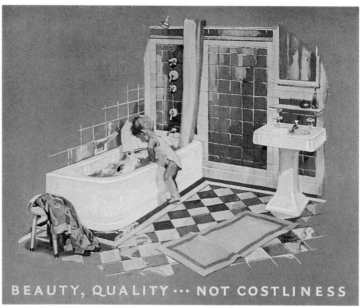

BEAUTY, QUALITY ··· NOT COSTLINESS

A 1925 advertisement. "There's many a ship that goes to sea in a tub of Kohler Ware. And there's many a sailor lad who grows up on good terms with fresh water—and soap, too—thanks to bathrooms made inviting by those fine fixtures..."

A 1926 advertisement. "When that boy of yours 'takes all day' in the bathroom, you merely realize more acutely the importance of having enough bathrooms to go around."

A 1926 ad run in the *Saturday Evening Post*, *Liberty*, *Literary Digest*, and *House and Garden*. "The great national game itself is no more truly a national institution than is the American bathroom."

A 1926 advertisement. "The lad who early learns something about that fine business of keeping clean and fit is well started on the road to manliness."

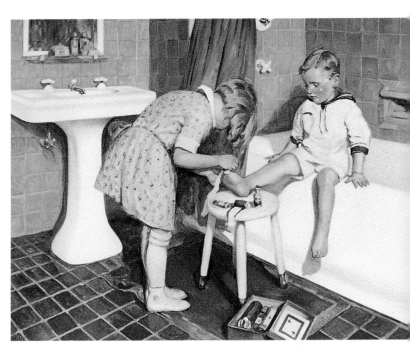

A 1927 advertisement. "You may be pleased to find that Kohler Plumbing Fixtures ... cost no more than any comparable ware."

# Color Charm
## Enters the Bathroom

♦

**KOHLER OF KOHLER**
*Plumbing Fixtures in Color*

Kohler was one of the first to perfect color matching technology, enabling it to produce enameled cast-iron tubs and porcelain sinks and toilet bowls that all matched. The company introduced its first five colors in 1927.

**Above:** The new paneled Mayfair tub and Bellaires lavatory, both in Autumn Brown with octagonal, gold-plated fittings.
**Right:** Spring Green Mayfair bath with gold-plated octachrome fittings and Fairfax dressing table lavatory with gold-plated faucet, supplies, and legs, plus matching bench.

Free-standing Imperator Bath with exposed top supply and secret drain fitting, and Belmore lavatory with lift-drain fitting, both in Horizon Blue.

Lavender Imperator Bath with combination shower, Belmore lavatory, and Rockbourne toilet.

Old Ivory Imperator Bath, Standish vitreous china lavatory, and Rockbourne toilet.

Kohler launched another advertising campaign in 1928, again featuring commissioned oil paintings to show off the new colorful bathroom fixtures. "It is the beauty of the complete color ensemble, now made possible for the first time by Kohler plumbing fixtures in color."

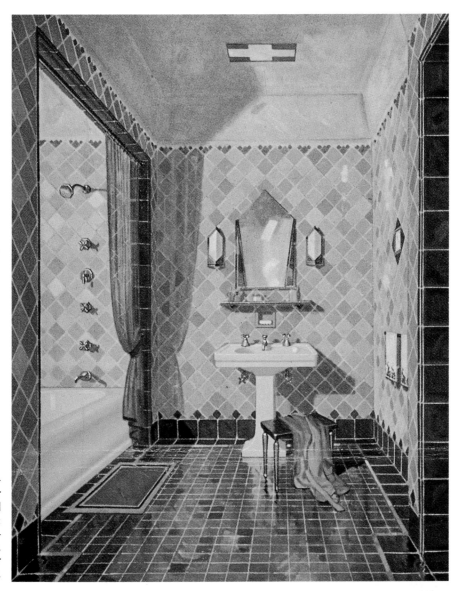

A 1929 advertisement lists costs for ready-to-install colored fittings: Lavatories, $35-800; bath tubs, $70-500; water closets, $60-150.

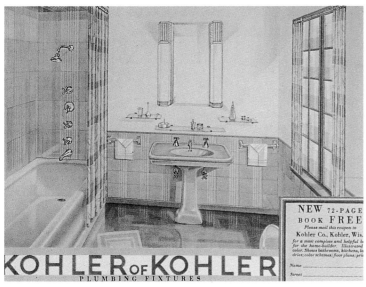

In a tradition that would carry through the current day, Kohler commissioned top designers to create bathrooms using the company's fixtures. Here a 1929 advertisement features a design by architect Ely Jacques Kahn, who also designed the following bathroom.

Kohler blows its own horn, announcing the incorporation of its fixtures in a design by architect Ely Jacques Kahn for the New York Metropolitan Museum of Art's exhibition on *American Industrial Art* in 1929. Note that the fixtures are black—a color that won't find popularity on the market for almost four decades.

A 1929 advertisement announces new colors for Kohler fixtures—"delicate but permanent, blue, green, ivory, brown, lavender, gray."

An April, 1929 advertisement in *Better Homes and Gardens*. "The loveliest of bathrooms, nowadays, are being created with Kohler Colorware."

An August, 1929 ad in *Liberty*. "The Viceroy bath, Filmore lavatory, and Rockbourne closet in Old Ivory, a favorite Kohler color."

# Promoting Clean Family Values

While targeting the house-proud home decorators, Kohler also went in for the big, industrial clients. Here they boast about the K of K Tuskolite closet seats. To prove their strength, this 1930 illustration shows a 185-pound man standing on one wing of the seat while a wedge passes from under it, over the other. The seats were also sold in white, color, or Sea Pearl finish.

Homeowners could now get all the guidance they needed about incorporating state-of-the-art bathrooms into their homes. Kohler Co. published numerous brochures and pamphlets in the 1930s offering room design ideas, especially for that "lavette." Kohler was on a mission to show Americans how to transform all those "unused spaces," like the space under the stairs or that dormer room upstairs, or that big closet off the bedroom, into convenient bathrooms that would improve family harmony. In addition to pushing these fairly costly remodeling projects, the company was also doing a hard sell on dental lavatories—small sinks that would aid children in the quest for healthier teeth and gums.

Kohler continued its family oriented advertising. This painting was used on the cover of a 1930 publication that promoted the idea of careful planning and quality goods "for better living."

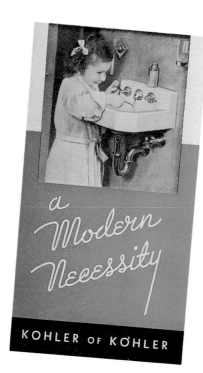

*a Modern Necessity*

KOHLER OF KOHLER

Kohler began promoting the installation and use of "dental lavatories" in the 1930s. These small sinks were mounted low so that "toothpaste or powder, brush and glass" were always at a children's fingertips, and visually accessible as a reminder. Moreover, they were supposed to "double bathroom usefulness" because while a child was brushing, dad could be shaving at the larger sink.

Above plan is laid out for a spacious bath, with the dental lavatory, shower stall, and dressing table optional. By omitting dental lavatory and shower stall, the plan can be condensed as shown below.

In 1936, Kohler offered free bathroom plans, packed with its products. In this plan, the dental lavatory, shower stall, and dressing table are optional.

This bathroom layout from Kohler offered a strategy for incorporating dormer windows into bathroom design. Such wings as shown on the house in the bottom left "are often not used above the first floor except for storage, and might well be transformed into baths and dressing rooms."

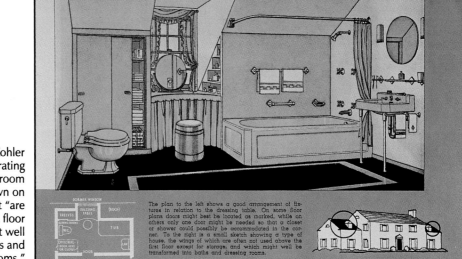

The plan to the left shows a good arrangement of fixtures in relation to the dressing table. On some floor plans doors might best be located as marked, while on others only one door might be needed so that a closet or shower could possibly be accommodated in the corner. To the right is a small sketch showing a type of house, the wings of which are often not used above the first floor except for storage, and which might well be transformed into baths and dressing rooms.

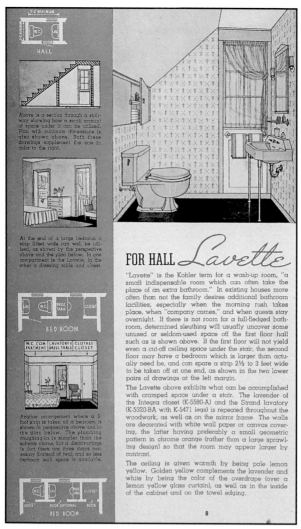

Kohler also promoted the "lavette," now known as the powder room, urging people to transform bedroom closets and spaces under stairs into "a small indispensable room which can often take the place of an extra bathroom."

The "Kohler Niedecken leak-proof shower for homes, apartments, hotels, schools, clubs, hospitals, gymnasiums" came on the market in 1937. Being of one piece, it was only practical for new construction projects.

The Kohler Cosmopolitan tub and matching fixtures in the color Tuscan are featured in this room design from 1938.

"A good example of what can be done with medium-priced fixtures." A 1938 design in Peachblow.

"For dad and his growing sons, this room should offer excellent suggestions." A 1938 design.

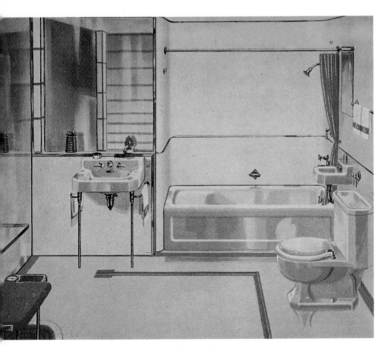

A Spring Green bathroom design from 1938 featuring the Metric bath with recessed seat.

"In this bathroom, which was 8 inches too wide for a 5.5-foot bath, 4 inch end fillers not only take up the extra space but provide valuable shelf space." A 1938 design.

"The single, modest bathroom serving a household of two adults and two children, must meet a variety of qualifications." This bathroom design from 1939 incorporates a disappearing step to help children reach the sink.

A four-fixture bathroom from 1939. Note the towel hamper/seat beside the tub, a common feature in American homes through the 1960s.

A lavette, now known as a powder room, with Peachblow colored Strand lavatory and Bolton toilet.

A Rouge Westchester lavatory is teamed with a white Cosmopolitan bath and Wellworth toilet in this budget-conscious 1939 design.

# Planning for a Post-War Boom

Like everyone else, Kohler went into war production during the early 1940s. But it did so with a vision into the future, into times of peace and prosperity when everyone would be building new homes and furnishing them with Kohler fixtures.

In a campaign targeted largely toward the wives left home alone, Kohler urged people to begin planning that post-war home now—and to leave plenty of room in their designs for quality fixtures.

In 1941, Kohler was urging people to plan with this booklet of ideas and a line of eight colors in plumbing fixtures. "Present day plumbing is functional and forthright. It is straight of line and clean of detail. It is neither Georgian or Victorian, French Provincial, nor Early American, but in a house or apartment of any period it is a handsome essential." The booklet included the following five design ideas.

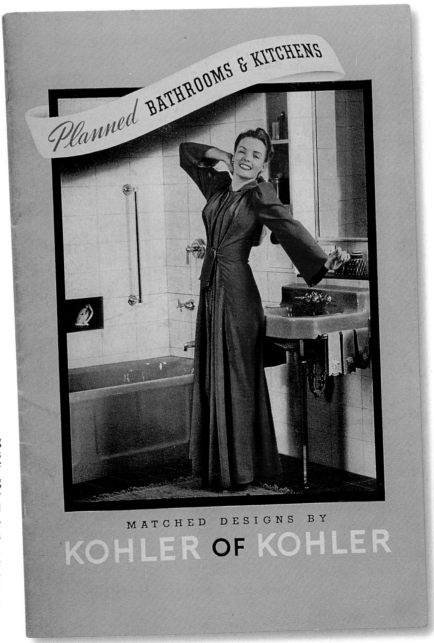

In this bathroom the fixtures are grouped closely to escape two inward swinging doors on the facing wall. Also, all the hot water outlets are located on the same inside wall to save on piping and protect from freezing. A Kohler Compact radiator is located under the window to ward off cold.

Again, pipe is saved by concentrating water outlets on one wall. An end wall for the bath/shower forms a booth for the toilet.

A spacious, square bath and dressing room features a recessed niche over the tub, an offset ledge above the lavatory, and built-in shelves and cupboards. Burgundy and white tile contrast with Cerulean Blue colored Cosmopolitan tub, Jamestown lavatory, Walcot dental lavatory, and Placid toilet.

The design above is modified using the lower-priced Channel toilet and excluding the dental lavatory, all in Tuscan, offset by blue linoleum walls.

A lavette with Peachblow Strand lavatory and Integra toilet.

Kohler offered the Potomac Set during World War II. It "saves critical materials, costs less, yet receives the same care in manufacture for which Kohler is known." In this 1942 *Saturday Evening Post* advertisement, Kohler addressed those "building homes for large worker groups, remodeling or planning plant expansion."

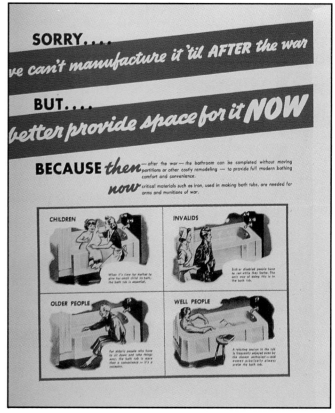

In a 1943 booklet, Kohler apologized for not being able to "manufacture it 'til after the war, but better provide space for it now." The brochure advises that sick or disabled people need to rest while they bathe, and that "women practically always prefer the bath tub" to a shower.

*Big Brother is Away*

It's up to the boys and girls at home to help take care of the bathroom – for essential materials – iron, brass, zinc, lead, copper, chromium, rubber – from which bathroom fixtures and fittings are made – are helping big brother win the war. Kohler plumbing fixtures are produced today only for war housing, war industries, hospitals, and military uses – and of non-critical materials. Kohler Co. is devoting its facilities to intensive production of implements of war, arming our forces on the ground, in the air, on and under the sea. Take care of your Kohler plumbing fixtures and fittings. Make your bathroom last. Kohler Co. Established in 1873. Kohler, Wisconsin.

**HERE'S HOW**
• Shut off faucets fully but without using unnecessary force.
• Keep all surfaces clean and drains open.
• Have your plumber make periodical inspections of your bathroom, kitchen and laundry plumbing equipment.
★ BUY UNITED STATES WAR BONDS ★

# KOHLER OF KOHLER
PLUMBING FIXTURES AND FITTINGS · HEATING EQUIPMENT · ELECTRIC PLANTS

"Kohler Co. is devoting its facilities to intensive production of implements of war, arming our forces on the ground, in the air, on and under the sea. Take care of your Kohler plumbing fixtures and fittings. Make your bathroom last." This 1943 *Saturday Evening Post* ad advised people to clean their plumbing fixtures, turn faucets off fully, but not forcefully, and have plumbing equipment inspected regularly.

"New advances in distinctive, practical design mark the bathroom and kitchen fixtures created by Kohler for your post-war home." A picture from a 1945 *Saturday Evening Post* advertisement promoting the free booklet, *Planned Bathrooms and Kitchens*.

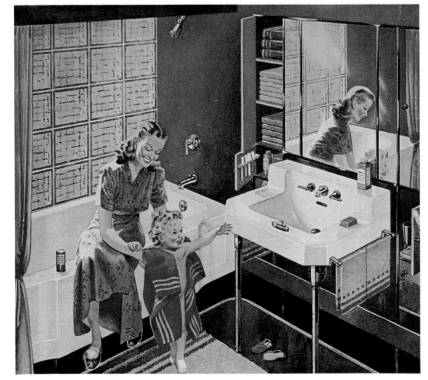

"Care of your family's health, training for life-long habits of cleanliness, pride in the facilities you depend upon to serve such important ends—put these high among the practical considerations in your home planning." A 1945 advertisement.

# BATHROOMS and KITCHENS by KOHLER OF KOHLER

Dad is back and Kohler is back in business. This is the cover from a booklet of design ideas offered by Kohler in 1947, including the following two illustrations.

This design features the 5-foot, 6-inch Cosmopolitan Bench Bath, Triton shower and bath fitting with dial mixer, and Chesapeake lavatory.

Promoting white fixtures including the 5-foot Cosmopolitan Bench Bath and Gramercy lavatory.

Peachblow fixtures and rosy cheeks—Kohler continues its colorful advertising campaign now two decades old in 1948. The inset shows a first-floor washroom with Kohler Strand lavatory that "takes little space, adds permanent value to your home, simplifies child training, and provides convenience for guests."

From a 1948 advertisement.

From a 1948 advertisement.

From a 1949 advertisement.

# Creating a Market by Design

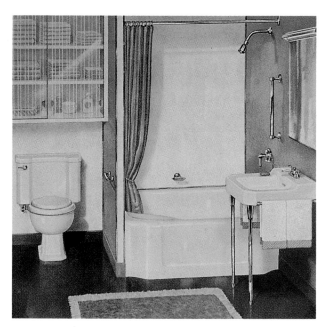

In these times of prosperity and growth, Kohler worked to expand its market by creating a desire for bigger, more beautiful bathrooms, and more of them. For the most part, Kohler advertising and promotional literature concentrated on design, and any people incorporated into the picture were used to illustrate domestic harmony. Toward the end of the decade, Kohler began to expand this idea to incorporate the element of glamour for women in their baths, a hint of things to come.

Times Square enamel bath, a new 4 x 4 foot showering bath, is featured in a bathroom design. The new shape is acclaimed by Kohler because it leaves extra space in small rooms for toilets or sinks. Also shown are Chesapeake lavatory and Channel siphon jet toilet, all in Tuscan.

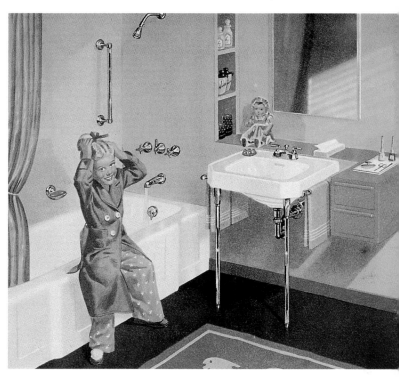

"Am I glad I live here!" From a 1950 *Saturday Evening Post* advertisement.

A first-floor washroom featuring the Strand lavatory and Bolton reverse trap toilet in Peachblow.

"Imagine me wanting to take a bath!" From a 1950 *Saturday Evening Post* advertisement.

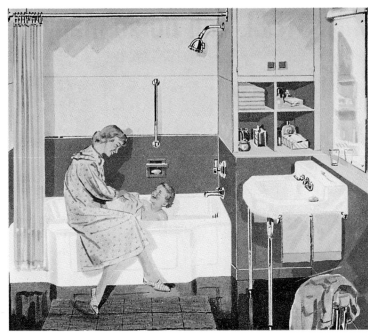

"Definition of a good bath." From a 1950 *Saturday Evening Post* advertisement for the Cosmopolitan Bench Bath.

A 1953 ad featuring the Cosmopolitan Bench Bath and the Hampton lavatory.

An advertising booklet for lavatory cabinets with composition tops.

The Mayflower square bath with oval basin, 48 x 44 inches, is introduced in a 1958 booklet.

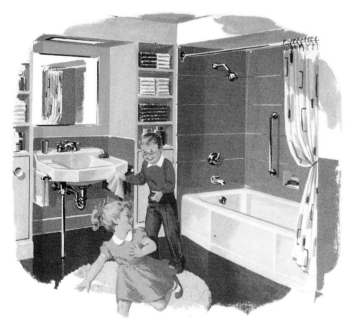

In 1958, Kohler illustrated a design plan incorporating this space-saving, 5-foot-long Minocqua bathtub.

Another small tub, the Standish (42 x 36 inches), was showcased in this 1958 design.

First aid to Beauty

New Kohler fittings of distinguished style and quality unite with Kohler fixtures to make the beautifying and hygienic use of water easy, safe, pleasing.

The new fittings, Constellation Series, combine fresh harmony of design with reliability for the exacting requirements of water-flow control. They fit the hand comfortably and respond to finger pressure. Beneath the jewel-bright chromium-plating they are made entirely of brass, the most durable and serviceable metal for plumbing fittings.

Fixtures in refreshing Spruce Green — the Piedmont vitreous china lavatory set in a convenient dressing-table top, and the graceful, enameled-iron Mayflower bath — are among the many Kohler types and sizes, all with new fittings expressly designed for them.

Consult your Kohler dealer. Write for booklet 23-A. KOHLER CO. Established 1873 KOHLER, WIS.

KOHLER OF KOHLER

A touch of glamour was added for this 1958 ad, which ran in *American Home, Better Homes & Gardens, New Homes Guide, Saturday Evening Post,* and *House Beautiful.*

Modern as tomorrow

are today's fixtures by Kohler

*The new Dynametric bath . . . the new Radiant lavatory*

And introducing them . . . the modern young matron, thrilled with her Kohler bathroom.

The Dynametric . . . balanced and graceful design . . . symmetrically enlarged bathing area for greater comfort, wide and flat for safety . . . gently sloped end for lounging ease . . . wide corner ledges for bath accessories.

The Radiant . . . circular with a deep bowl . . . fitted into a cabinet to make grooming convenient.

Sparkling enamel, in color or white, is wedded to the durable cast iron. And the chrome-plated Constellation faucets and fittings are all brass, the metal least subject to wear and corrosion.

Give your old bathroom the new look. And if you're adding a new bathroom . . . and convenience and value . . . to your present home, or choosing fixtures for a new home, consult your Kohler dealer. Write for booklet 14-C.

KOHLER CO. Established 1873 KOHLER, WIS.

KOHLER OF KOHLER

ENAMELED IRON AND VITREOUS CHINA PLUMBING FIXTURES • BRASS FITTINGS • ELECTRIC PLANTS • AIR-COOLED ENGINES • PRECISION CONTROLS

"Modern as tomorrow." A 1959 ad.

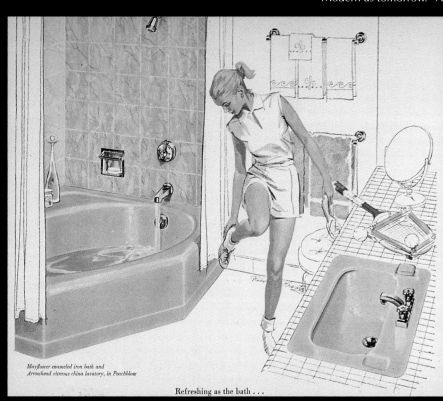

*Mayflower enameled iron bath and Arrowhead vitreous china lavatory, in Peachblow*

Refreshing as the bath . . .

A 1959 ad featuring the Mayflower bath and Arrowhead lavatory.

This and the following five design ideas were offered in a 1959 booklet from Kohler. This layout features fixtures in the Suez Tan color matched with green ceramic tile in bath, metallic wallpaper, and vinyl floor.

7'-0"x14'-0"

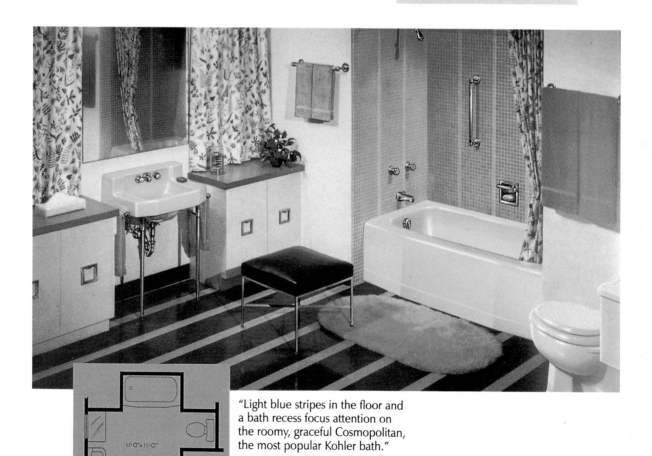

11'-0"x11'-0"

"Light blue stripes in the floor and a bath recess focus attention on the roomy, graceful Cosmopolitan, the most popular Kohler bath."

— 29 —

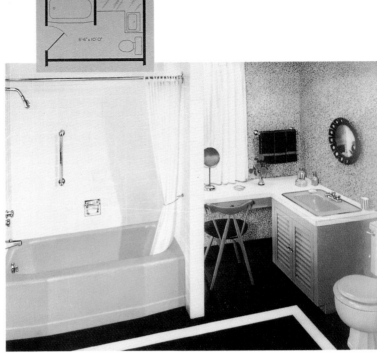

"Pleasing Budget Bathroom" features space-saving, easy-to-clean enameled cast iron fixtures—the Minocqua bath and Chester lavatory, with vitreous china Trylon toilet, all in Argent gray.

"The clean, luminous white of bath recess, cabinet top and chintz curtains appears even whiter against the midnight black floor and towels. The multi-colored wallpaper, dove gray cabinet and Swedish chair add decorative charm."

"This is what the decorator did to this bathroom—using Spruce Green fixtures, strong blues in floor and cabinet, brilliant white in counter-top and shag rug."

"Here the Cerulean Blue closet and lavatory are accented in a simple room of yellow and white, with touches of blue in accessories."

# Bold Moves for Market Dominance

The 1960s started out all innocence, with ads portraying hometown girls and happy moms. That changed drastically in 1965, when the company launched a new plumbing product and advertising campaign called "The Bold Look of Kohler." Bathroom and kitchen sinks were presented to the American public in a highly charged campaign that had an immediate effect on the company's popularity. The company was right on top of a rapidly changing market, keeping up with tastes that swung from the by now institutional pastels to bright yellow, bold orange and red, and the decade's characteristic Avocado green. Kohler helped lead the way, contracting top designers and cooperating with leading magazines to incorporate Kohler fixtures in state-of-the-art, ultra-bold designs that—viewed today—scream '60s.

"Dad and mom must agree, 'it's the most' to have a second bathroom for their favorite daughter—and bathroom emancipation for themselves." A 1960 ad run in *The Saturday Evening Post, Better Homes & Gardens, American Home, House Beautiful's Building Manual,* and *House & Garden's Book of Building.*

"Twins are nice...so are twin bathrooms with fixtures by Kohler of Kohler." A 1961 advertisement.

*Avoid family blowups!*
*. . . add a Powder Room*

**KOHLER** OF **KOHLER**

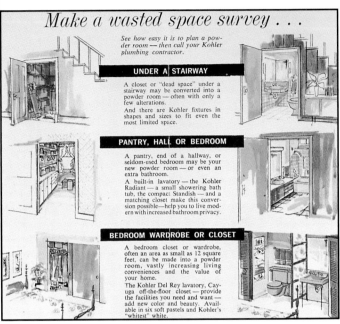

*Make a wasted space survey . . .*

See how easy it is to plan a powder room — then call your Kohler plumbing contractor.

**UNDER A STAIRWAY**

A closet or "dead space" under a stairway may be converted into a powder room — often with only a few alterations.

And there are Kohler fixtures in shapes and sizes to fit even the most limited space.

**PANTRY, HALL OR BEDROOM**

A pantry, end of a hallway, or seldom-used bedroom may be your new powder room — or even an extra bathroom.

A built-in lavatory — the Kohler Radiant — a small showering bath tub, the compact Standish — and a matching closet make this conversion possible — help you to live modern with increased bathroom privacy.

**BEDROOM WARDROBE OR CLOSET**

A bedroom closet or wardrobe, often an area as small as 12 square feet, can be made into a powder room, vastly increasing living conveniences and the value of your home.

The Kohler Del Rey lavatory, Cayuga off-the-floor closet — provide the facilities you need and want — add new color and beauty. Available in six soft pastels and Kohler's "whitest" white.

This 1962 brochure was part of Kohler's mission to expand the number of bathrooms in American homes, and furnish them!

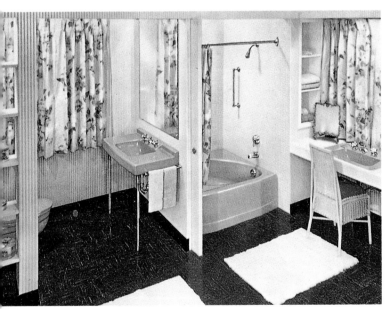

This and the following seven pictures were design ideas offered in a booklet by Kohler with the message that, "with enough Kohler bathrooms, there's no place like home." This design features the Champlain toilet, Valcour lavatory, Mayflower bath, and Carvel lavatory, all in Spruce Green.

"Accent on Beauty." The Gramercy lavatory, Dynametric bath, and Bolton toilet, all in Peachblow.

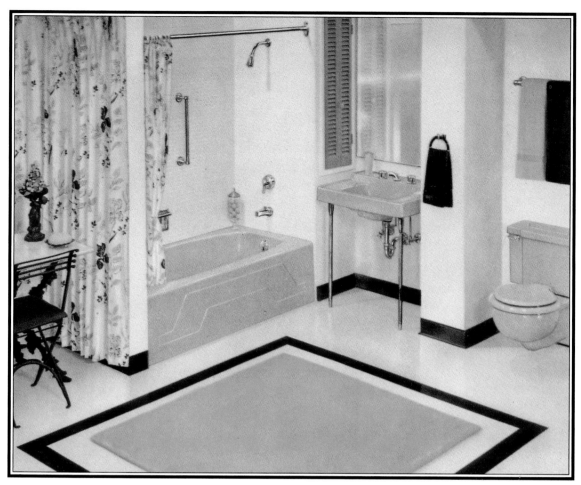

"A Bathroom with Everything." The Dynametric bath, Chesapeake lavatory, and Cayuga toilet, all in Cerulean Blue with all-brass fittings. This toilet was designed to make mopping up easier, inspiring the company's oft-used slogan—"Off-the-floor lightens a chore."

"A Practical Plan." The Arrowhead lavatory, Dynametric bath, and Bolton closet, all in Suez Tan.

"Low Cost Luxury." The Minocqua bath, Hampton lavatory, and the ever-popular Wellworth reverse trap closet, all in Sunrise.

"A Step-saver Washroom ... Practical for family use, yet liberally treated with touches of luxury.... New home plans should include a wash-room—existing homes can be modernized by converting unused space—a pantry, a large closet, a hallway, the space under a stairway."

"A Space-saver Bathroom ... The secret is the compact (42 x 36 inch) Standish bath." Also shown are the Del Ray lavatory and the Wellworth toilet, all in Suez Tan.

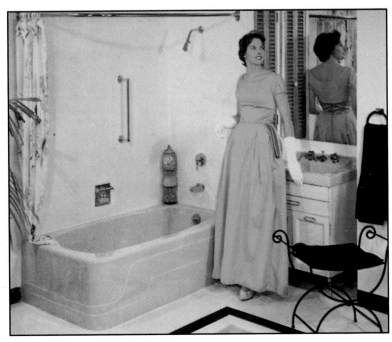

"The Champion of Bathing Comfort." The Dynametric is offered in three sizes, including the 5-foot corner design pictured.

"Kohler makes the kind of bath tub you can really feel comfortable with." A 1963 advertisement run in *American Home*.

**Above & Right:** In a prelude to its later surrealist advertisements, a 1963 brochure on Kohler toilets featured the products in unnatural nature settings.

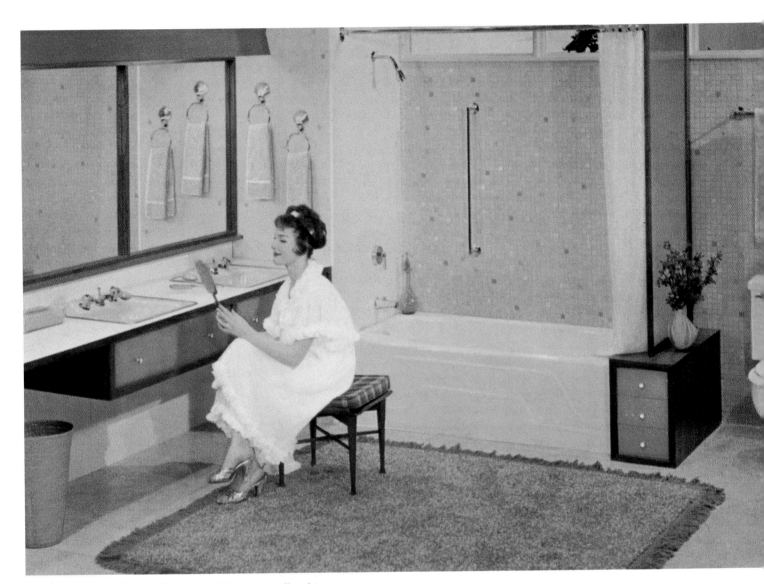

This and the following three design ideas were offered in a 1963 Kohler catalog. Here Sunrise yellow fixtures and orange trim lend this room its cutting edge '60s charm.

A luxury bath featuring the Valencia bidet, Champlain closet, Caxton lavatories, and Dynametric tub.

The Cloud Grey vanity featured in this picture was a Kohler offering.

"A Step-saver powder room" with Brookline lavatory and Wellworth toilet.

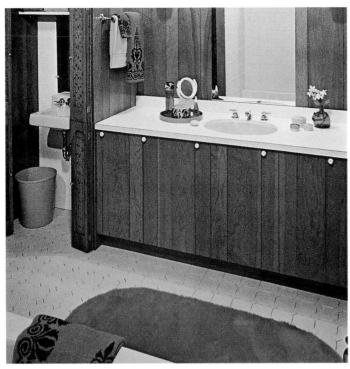

This and the following five designer ideas were offered in a 1964 catalog from Kohler. This design was by *House & Garden* magazine using Sunrise Yellow Kohler fixtures and pecan paneling.

The California Bathroom, designed by *California Home* magazine using Peachblow Kohler fixtures.

Early American Bathroom designed by *American Home* magazine using Suez Tan Kohler fixtures, cherry paneling and cabinets, and red bandanna wallpaper and shower curtain.

French Provincial Bathroom created by a Kohler staff designer using Cerulean Blue fixtures.

Guest Bathroom designed by *House Beautiful* magazine using Argent-colored Kohler fixtures.

Remodeled bathroom designed by *Home Modernizing Guide* using white Kohler fixtures.

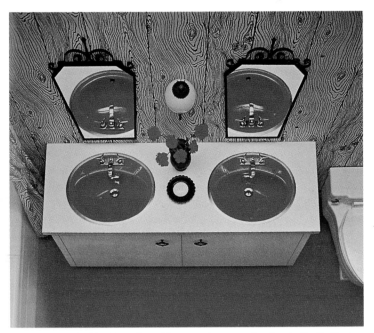

In 1965, Kohler introduced its new Accent color line in its Radiant, Farmington, and Tahoe lavatories to coordinate with existing colors. Here Antique Red lavatories are paired with white and a "bathroom becomes about the most exciting thing you have ever seen."

Expresso is paired with Suez Tan "for a warm, rich look."

Citron is paired with Sunrise Yellow "in absolute harmony."

The quietly daring combination of Jade and Cerulean Blue."

Another introduction in 1965 was the slip-resistant bath tub bottom, advertised here with the company's first nearly nude adult. Much more to follow...

These creative ads ran in 1965, showcasing Kohler fixtures not within bathroom settings, but as stage props in exotic fantasies.

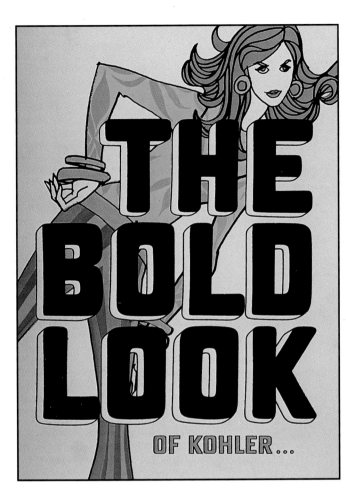

# THE BOLD LOOK
## OF KOHLER...

The bold look woman made funky fashion statements reflecting the mod age.

Avocado's partner in decorating, Tiger Lily orange, is introduced to Kohler's line in 1968.

Here the bold look woman puts her stamp of approval on a new color from Kohler, one that was to dominate the times—Avocado.

A new luxury bathroom fixture from Kohler—the Lady Fair Shampoo Basin—was introduced in 1968. The spray arm could be used for shampooing, as well as for bathing babies who had more room in the lavatory due to a "swing-away spout."

This and the following three powder room designs were offered in a booklet put out by Kohler in 1968. This photo stresses the Antique Red self-rimming lavatory basin and Flair faucet fitting with white acrylic handles.

The Lady Fair Shampoo Basin in Avocado gives this powder room "Real Convenience."

This design suggests that homeowners turn clothes closets off their master bedrooms into convenient half-baths.

"Put out your best towels and show off Kohler fixtures in Spruce Green. Strand lavatory basin and low-silhouette toilet are ideal for a narrow room."

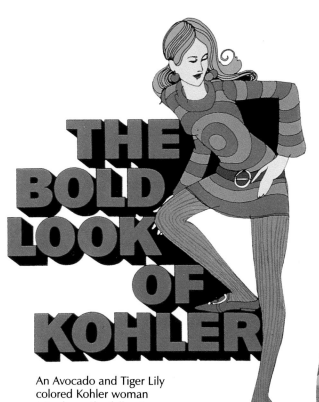

# THE BOLD LOOK OF KOHLER

An Avocado and Tiger Lily colored Kohler woman introduces the following nine design ideas in a 1968 booklet from Kohler.

YOUR GUIDE TO QUALITY PLUMBING FIXTURES

"Daring, bright and bold. Away with timid bathrooms."

"Wild Tiger Lily with Avocado" and gold electroplated Flair facet fittings. In the center is the Caribbean bathtub—6 feet long and a yard wide.

"Master Bathroom. Subtle blending of colors for an aura of elegance."

"Accent Bathroom." Farmington lavatory in Antique Red, Cerulean Blue Dynametric bathtub, Champlain closet, and Valencia bidet.

"Warm Colors in Fanciful Decor." Design features a new color for fixtures—Harvest Gold—"at home in almost any turn of the color wheel, including electric blue and rakish red."

"The Pink of Peachblow. You've always dreamed of an elegant home? Then here are plumbing fixtures in gentle Peachblow that befit an elegant setting."

"Begin bold, with gold. Choose Kohler's Amber Flair faucet fittings."

"Instantly Inviting. . . Blueberry basins come up bright against a muted mustard counter top." The Kohler Caribbean bathtub was "designed to let you carpet right up the side."

"Bath and Beauty Center. Where lives the girl who could resist wanting a bathroom like this?"

This and the following three designs were offered in an "Idea Portfolio" published by Kohler in 1968.

Here the Caribbean tub's side is papered to match the surrounding walls.

Accent towels in bittersweet and Spanish straw compliment an Avocado tub in the foreground.

Floral greens and blues for a subdued color effect.

A new color from Kohler—New Orleans Blue. The 6-foot-long Caribbean bathtub is sunken and surrounded with a soft carpet in contrasting gold. This and the following two ideas were published in a Kohler product guide for 1969.

"A lovely bathroom in Harvest Gold." The Guardian bathtub offers grip rails and Safe-guard® textured bottom. Fittings are gold electroplated.

"Bouquets for Avocado." This design showcases Kohler's "go-with-everything color."

# Setting Standards of Excellence and Luxury

By the end of the decade, Kohler's relentless "Bold Look" advertising campaign and massive product line expansion boosted it to the number one position in the plumbing industry. Kohler was an innovator in a market that was ever changing. As was the nature of the bathroom during the 1970s, transforming from a private sanctum set aside for the business of cleanliness to a place of leisure. Tubs swelled drastically in size, and started accommodating more and more people. And, in a sign of innocence lost, models bared almost all for the camera in suggestive advertisements that underlined the Bold Look of Kohler. Besides eye-catching ads, Kohler was making its mark with products that blew the competition away. Status goods like the fully enclosed Environment™ didn't become best sellers, but they established Kohler as the luxury company that offered the very best.

Kohler kicked off 1970 with a new color—Mexican Sand—and a revisit to its stage-setting advertising concept. This ad papered the *Better Homes & Gardens, House & Garden,* and *House Beautiful* publications. "Own a walk-in work of art."

This Mexican Sand design concept was featured
on the cover of a 1970 Kohler catalog.

"Bathroom Reborn." A home from the 1870s, bathroom for the 1970s." New Orleans Blue tub and
Bolton Aqua-Vent toilet are mixed with Blueberry
accent twin Tahoe lavatory basins in this 1970 design.

A new color, Fresh Green, was
introduced in this 1971 brochure.

# THE BOLD LOOK OF KOHLER

The Bold Look Girl sports a new image in a 1971 brochure introducing Kohler design concepts, including the following seven ideas.

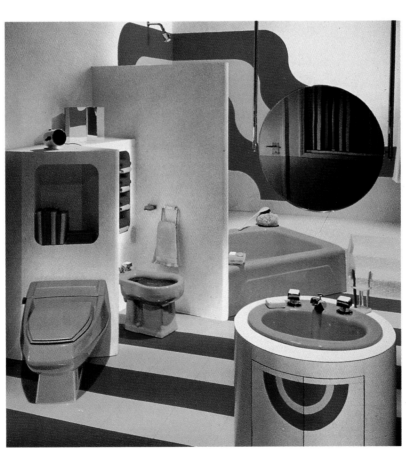

"Look what you can do with the 'blah' bath!" A concept featuring Fresh Green fixtures including the Pennington lavatory with Alterna fittings, the Rochelle toilet, and square-shaped Bradford tub.

"Here's a bathroom for the 1970s, spacious and attractive." Cerulean Blue fixtures, rough-sawn southern pine walls, and slate quarry tile floor, "bring the seashore to the door."

"Here's elegance in striking Antique Red and gentle Peachblow."

Four modest bathrooms proposed by Kohler with Farmington lavatories, Seaforth bathtubs, and Wellworth toilets.

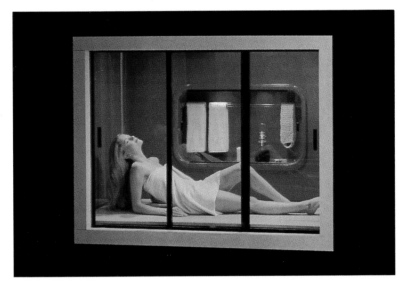

The 1978 Habitat offers a 50-minute cycle of sun, steam, and rain, using approximately forty-two gallons of water and four kilowatt hours of electricity. Small heat lamps in enclosed chamber keep towels toasty.

The Kohler Whirlpool Baths of 1978 featured solid brass jets and fittings in brushed or polished chrome or 24-carat gold finishes. Pictured, the Infinity-Bath™ measures 5 x 42 feet, with a 20-inch depth. Made of durable acrylic, it came in twelve colors including the Sequoia shown, and here it is outfitted with twin showers and a master control console in brushed 24-karat gold electroplate.

Top of the line luxury—the Environment, with Baja sun, tropic rain and spring showers, jungle steam, and Chinook winds. The enclosure includes four heat lamps, four sun lamps, six 24-karat gold finished spray heads, a steam generator, two warm air circulating systems, a hand-held shower, an air-filled comfort pad with pillow, a 20-inch porthole cabinet with shelves, a 30-inch porthole window, a silk-screened painting on back-lighted Lucite panel, and a stereo system with radio and cassette tape player.

# Hydro-Whirl
## from Kohler

For the common man, or woman, Kohler also introduced the low-cost Hydro-Whirl, an adapter that you could install to add bubbles to your bath. The luxury whirlpool tubs were on their way.

For the more social bather, Kohler started introducing a series of spas. Here is a family scene in the Spa Ville D'eau in Aspen Green, designed to accommodate four to six people.

Other 1978 introductions by Kohler were the Nostalgia line of fixtures including a turn-of-the-century Vintage toilet with elevated tank, pull chain, oak seat and cover, the Birthday Bath with rolled rim and ball-and-claw feet, and the Chablis pedestal lavatory, all shown with Antique faucets.

In the coming years, Kohler ads featured party scenes in the spa. Here four enjoy a Sequoia-colored Super Spa®.

Country Grey "because there's a little bit of country in all of us." Here shown with the Steeping Bath Whirlpool in the foreground.

Evergreen is featured on the Steeping Bath Whirlpool and Man's Lav, with complimentary Aspen Green San Raphael Water-Guard toilet.

In 1972, Kohler introduced Black Black, shown here with some of the company's top products: The Bath, a 5.5 x 7-foot fiberglass bathing oval, the Lady Vanity, Rochelle toilet, Caravelle bidet, and Man's Lav.

The "remarkable uncolor" on a Caribbean bathtub and Pompton toilet, set in a flashy zebra-stripe setting.

This and the following four designs were offered in a 1972 booklet from Kohler.

The all-purpose room opens onto a private garden patio on one side, a health center on the other. Fixtures include the Caribbean bath in New Orleans Blue with Alterna polished chromium fittings, a Fresh Green Rochelle toilet, and white Farmington self-rimming lavatory.

In this and the following design, Kohler gives a nod to other great designers. "Earthtones" dominate this design, inspired by the "Pussywillow" pattern of the J. P. Stevens sheeting fabric used as wall covering.

"Teenage Bathroom" features a Toulouse Lautrec poster by Peter Max.

"Man's Room." Bathing conveniences at every turn, plus a refreshment area with Addison bar sink in Tiger Lily.

"Kohler wants you to have fun creating a bath or powder room that reflects your own personality."

## The SWINGER

This faucet wasn't the greatest innovation by man, but the name is a reflection on major changes in society. Kohler's advertising, likewise, was changing drastically, from rosy cheeked children, to more cheeky content. The models shed all in a look that was, well, the Bold Look of Kohler.

No more fighting over the bathroom with the Infinity-Bath Whirlpool from Kohler. "Luxurious for one. Spacious for two."

Another naked model in Habitat for one of the early surrealist ads by Kohler in 1978.

# Pink Champagne

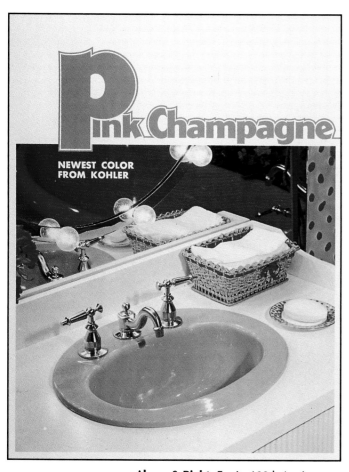

NEWEST COLOR
FROM KOHLER

# The Birthday bath

Another Great Bathroom Idea
from KOHLER

**Above & Right:** For its 100th Anniversary in 1973, Kohler introduced the Birthday Bath, and a new color—Pink Champagne.

## THE BOLD LOOK OF KOHLER

The changed look of the Bold Look Girl in 1973.

A bathroom in the new Pink Champagne color.

Kohler teamed up with other manufacturers to create this and the following three "Uncommon bath" design ideas offered in a 1973 Kohler leaflet. Here the keynote is Calico, from the Springmaid Bill Blass collection, a Monterey vanity by Connor, and counter laminate by Durabeauty.

The Gazebo Bath creates a latticed garden effect teamed up with Springmaid sheets in a coordinating plaid designed by Bill Blass with matching shower curtain, wall covering, and towels. The double vanity is topped by a Durabeauty plastic laminated counter and a Kohler shampoo center in Fresh Green.

The Rajah Bath is an oasis of luxury with a tented ceiling, wall covering, and shower curtain created with sheets in the Etching pattern designed by Bill Blass. The focal point of the room is Kohler's Birthday Bath in Black Black with gold electroplated Antique fittings. Also, there are Confetti Stripe accent towels from the Bill Blass collection and a triple vanity by Connor.

**Above:** The Japanese Bath with bamboo, quarry tile, and natural woods. The bathtub is fitted with a Kohler Raindrop personal shower to allow you to soap and rinse on the bathing platform prior to soaking, as is the Japanese custom. Bill Blass Grosgrain Ribbon towels are pictured, and the mat cover in the foreground is made from matching sheets.

**Left:** Kohler has been introducing Japanese bathing traditions to an American audience for more than two decades. Here, the earliest Steeping Bath allows one to bathe, while an adjacent pit offers a platform for advance showering.

In 1976 and '77, Kohler ran a series of ads presenting entire bathrooms in entirely unlikely situations, calling it "A Kohler Tour of America's Baths." This was the Key Largo ad: "Come to a private place in Kohler's pinks and reds. Designed especially for the free spirit in you."

"Cityscape. Pick up the beat of the city. Here, high above it all, tour a dream bath with plumbing fixtures in Black Black, Kohler's high fashion color."

"Desert Spring. A world of sun, sand, and eternal enchantment. Where warm earthtones complement Kohler's plumbing fixtures in rich Expresso."

# A KOHLER TOUR OF AMERICA'S BATHS

"Colonial Interlude. Featuring Kohler's newest color. Parchment. The off-white with character. A subtle decorator color that creates this mood of relaxation."

## You can't live in a perfect climate. But that doesn't mean you can't own one.

**Habitat™ by Kohler.**

Habitat is a remarkable addition to the series of Kohler environmental enclosures. It's designed to let you experience the soothing elements of warm Sun, refreshing Rain, and cleansing Steam, a delightful option. All within a single unit.

Habitat also gives you two conditioning elements, Ambience and Warm Breeze, to enhance the atmosphere. And warm the enclosure.

This is how it works. Select any element to begin your Habitat experience. When you're ready for a change, select another element... or let Habitat sequence automatically every 20 minutes. You can also add conditioning elements as you wish. Add warm breeze to sun, and you have a desert afternoon, buffed by light wind. Ambience and Rain create a bright summer shower.

The combinations seem endless. And so do the pleasures.

Habitat's suggested list price is $4700, plus freight, installation, and options.

For all its uniqueness, Habitat is water and energy efficient. A one hour sequence costs just about 25¢.

Learn more about Habitat. In the U.S. or Canada, look for your Kohler dealer in the Yellow Pages. Or send 50¢ to Kohler Co., Box EZ, Kohler, WI 53044.

Habitat, by Kohler. A climate you can own.

**The Bold Look of Kohler**

Though Kohler sells few Habitat™ units, the company is proud of the leadership position it has earned among competitors.

## For $10,000, you can feel like a million.

It can warm you. Tan you. Invigorate or refresh you. Cleanse you with billows of relaxing steam. And soothe you with warm, gentle winds.

It is Environment™ by Kohler. There has never been anything like it before.

Environment is a secluded retreat within your own home or office. The suggested list price for the base unit is $10,000. Installation and accessories not included. It offers the best elements of nature: Baja Sun, Tropic Rain, Jungle Steam, Spring Showers and Chinook Winds. Simply select the elements and the amount of time for each from the control panel. Choose your favorite kind of stereo music. Then step into the rich, hand crafted teak interior. And relax.

To give you complete peace of mind, you'll be delighted to know that Environment consumes only 22¢ per hour in water and energy during a normal cycle, based on national averages.

For more information, look for your Kohler dealer in the Yellow Pages. Or send $2.50 to ENVIRONMENT, DEPT. MC, KOHLER CO., KOHLER, WIS. 53044, for a beautifully illustrated brochure.

Environment, by Kohler. It'll make you feel like a million dollars.

**The Bold Look of Kohler**

Likewise, even fewer Environments are sold.

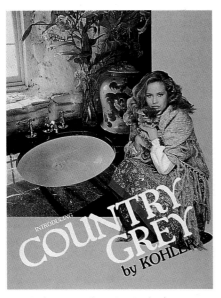

A Tobago fiberglass shower cove ties in with Country Grey Rochelle toilet and Caravelle bidet.

Styles were changing in the late 1970s, from bold colors to natural tones and peasant tastes. Kohler began to reemphasize Country Grey, here reintroducing it in a 1978 pamphlet that included the following two design ideas.

The Bath Whirlpool in Country Grey with dual Alterna Onyx faucets and other fittings in polished chromium.

From an uncharacteristic, but very attractive Country Grey toilet ad by Kohler—"Because every woman has two worlds. The one she lives in and the one she dreams in."

A design idea incorporating Aspen Green, one of the more
natural tones making its way to the forefront in 1979.

Pushing Swiss Chocolate, along with the
back-to-nature movement, in 1979.

It was new to some people in 1979 when Kohler
came out with this promotional brochure.

# Making Waves in the Advertising World

The 1980s were groundbreaking times for Kohler in the world of advertising. Starting out the decade with surrealist images that still haunt many people's minds, the company went on to promote visually stimulating ads that highlighted its products in unusual situations. More than the products, though, Kohler was out to establish its name.

Kohler entered the 1980s with its "At the edge of your imagination" series, some of the decade's most popular advertising, like this famous image promoting the company's toilets.

"Once upon a time, bathrooms were small, bathtubs were white, and bathing was a Spartan ritual. Times have changed!"

"At the edge of your imagination, a daring departure breaks all the rules. Trend. A superior faucet that is not expensive."

"At the edge of your imagination lies a new frontier of comfort. The Super Spa, 103 x 86.5 inches of sublimity."

"Not since *Singing in the Rain* has water been tapped with such classic style and grace."

"Leave it to the French to take something as simple as vanilla and give it spice. Make it richer, creamier, and tastier than it's been before. Leave it to Kohler to bring it to the bath."

"This, fellow citizen, is the newest state of pleasure. The Greek Bath by Kohler. Here geometry triumphs. The bath is but 4 feet long (fits in the space of a shower) yet its unique 22-inch depth assures comfort for any man of stature."

"Vanquish those dragons of the Age of the Commonplace. Live the graciousness of the American Georgian era when elegance and uniqueness were a way of life. A period represented by IV Georges Brass, Kohler's cast and richly turned brass faucets and accessories."

"Wild Rose, a bold high fashion Kohler color."

A design idea suited to the early 1980s customer. "Whether you are a worldwide traveler, a compulsive collector, or an amateur artist, here's a room setting that reflects the real you."

This and the following two color scheme ideas were offered by Kohler to tie in with its fiberglass bathing modules. Here the Barbados, with whirlpool and shower.

The Trinidad compact bathing module.

The Bimini compact unit fits through most doorways—ideal for remodeling, states Kohler.

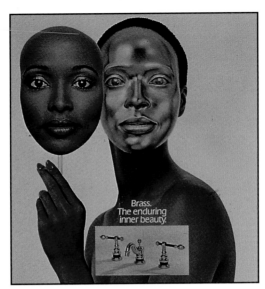

"Brass. The enduring inner beauty."

"Comfort is what the Greek Bath is all about. The Greek Bath is 22 inches deep. A bather 6 foot 4 inches can soak or enjoy a whirlpool bath. Integral armrests add to the relaxation."

"In the world of Kohler, form and function emerge triumphant. Here, the Flair II™ Faucet in cast brass."

"The first bath luxurious for one, spacious for two...The Infinity-Bath™ Whirlpool."

"Finally, a faucet that turns heads. The new Finesse™."

The emphasis on group soaks continued into the 1980s. This photo of the fiberglass Invitation Spa and the following four images were in a Spa brochure published by Kohler in 1985.

A picnic around the Essence Spa.

A private outdoor soak for two in the Tango Spa.

The Eternity Bath & Spa.

A ski vacation scene centered around the Spa Ville D'eau.

Talk about luxury, this was it in 1981. Still is. Kohler set itself up as the industry leader in the early 1970s with products like those pictured here. Kohler's two-person Infinity-Bath™ Whirlpool dominates a huge bathroom. Behind that are twin Castelle lavatories, San Raphael Water-Guard toilet, and San Tropéz bidet. To the right is Habitat, an environmental enclosure that offers cycles of warm sun, refreshing rain, and invigorating steam.

Eight people in a Kohler spa, with another woman enjoying an environmental enclosure in the background—this was the standard for luxury on the cover of a 1980 catalog of leisure products.

A 1981 brochure offered this and the following three design ideas that incorporated Kohler's latest colors. Here Wild Rose adorns the Caribbean Whirlpool bath, Le Gran and Castelle lavatories, Rochelle toilet, and Caravelle bidet. The Alterna Onyx faucets have a 24-karat brushed gold finish.

The new Swiss Chocolate color on the Super Bath Whirlpool, Pompton toilet, Caravelle bidet, Man's Lav, and Lady Vanity. Bravura faucets have a polished gold finish.

Aspen Green on the Rondelle lavatory with Antique faucet, Guardian bath, and Pompton toilet.

Georgian Splendor with the IV Georges Brass faucet and matching accessories on Chablis pedestal lavatory and Rochelle toilet.

"Streams of bubbles to massage your back, your feet, your soul. The new Hourglass-Bath® Bubble Massage.

**Above:** "Surround yourself with its grace. And vitality. The Kohler Arabesque™ pedestal lavatory in Innocent Blush™. Circled by design with an artful towel bar in a choice of finishes. Use with the sculptured Cirrus™ sheetflow faucet."

**Left:** "A new era for drawing the bath. The Kohler Autofill™ for the Infinity-Bath™ whirlpool."

ARTIST EDITIONS

In the mid-1980s, Kohler initiated a challenge to artists to create bold designs in bathroom fixtures. The one pictured is called Cactus Cutter™ by ceramic artist Art Nelson.

"For you, only silk and stone will do. The rich glow, the silken feel of IV Georges Brass™ faucet ... shown here with our black marble console table and Country™ Grey basin."

"Explore the luxurious, rejuvenating power of the Mandalay™ Teakwood Suite." A 1986 advertisement.

In the late 1980s, Kohler commissioned artists to incorporate their artwork into its products. The results were published in a series of magazine ads entitled *As I See It*. This one is *Another World*, color-saturated photography by Rebecca Blake.

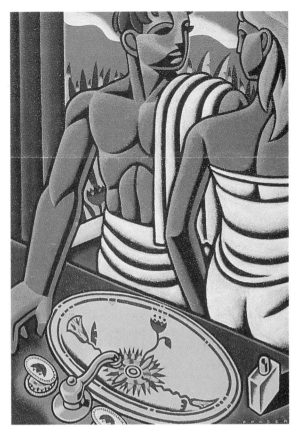

*The Morning After*, acrylic on
canvas by Douglas Fraser.

*Shaping the Flow*, air brush illustration/photography
by David Jonason/Ryszard Horowitz.

*Roughing It*, high-grain photography
by Gregory Heisler.

*Renaissance Redux*, Polaroid 20 x 24 Polacolor
photography by Joyce Tenneson.

# Form, Color, and Craftsmanship

Commissioning artists and teaming up with craftsmen and top quality manufacturers, Kohler has created a line of exclusive and highly impressive goods. Following is a small sampling of their "wow" line of bathroom wares.

An Artist Editions sink, the Terragon™ Lavatory in solid brass with Cygnet faucet.

Vessels™ Turnings with glazed underside of vitreous china, with Falling Water faucet.

Anatole™ Pedestal Lavatory,
shown with Antique faucet.

**Above and following two pages:** Kohler designs coordinate
bathroom suites, from the sink to the bidet and bath.

Ankara™ Vintage Countertop Lavatory, from the Artist Editions line, with matching Antique faucet with Ankara ceramic trim.

The Artist Editions Russian Teacup design takes its inspiration from the lavish Russian Imperial style, particularly a tea and coffee set crafted for Catherine the Great. Cobalt blue and gold are blended with jade accents on a background of White vitreous china to decorate an Anatole Pedestal Lavatory.

Artist Editions Provincial design on Vintage Countertop Lavatory.

Loon™, by artist Christel-Anthony Tucholke, interprets the bird's black markings on White vitreous china, including Chablis™ Pedestal Lavatory, Vintage Countertop Lavatory, and Wellington Toilet.

Islander™ features a tropical design based on authentic Haitian art, here on Cantata Countertop Lavatory, the handles of Taboret base faucet, and other accessories.

Isis™ design on Vintage Countertop Lavatory, handles of Antique faucet, and assorted accessories.

Calabria Artist Editions design on Revival Pedestal Lavatory, Vintage Bath,
Revival Two-piece Toilet, and Floor Container, against Chamois background.

Calabria design on lavatory and toilet against Timberline background.

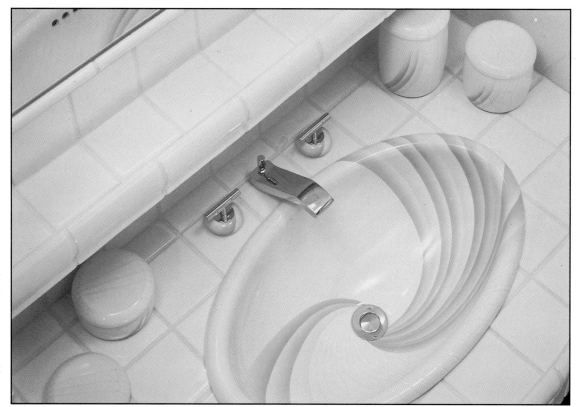

The Escapade™ Artist Editions design takes its inspiration from the swirls and delicate coloring of seashells, here on Vintage Countertop Lavatory, Taboret base faucet handles, and countertop accessories.

**Opposite & this page:** The English Trellis Artist Editions design was inspired by English chintz patterns. Here it is shown on the Portrait Countertop Lavatory, Antique faucet trim, and Vintage vitreous china bath base, along with complementary English Trellis decorative tile and Kohler solid color tiles. Likewise, the Portrait Toilet is adorned with English Trellis design.

**Left:** Alouette™ is a French country floral pattern, here shown on the Portrait Toilet, Portrait Wall-mount Lavatory, and Portrait Cistern. Also, the Alouette design has been applied to a matching toilet tissue holder and towel ring.

**Above & Left:** Peonies & Ivy Artist Editions design is applied to Undercounter Lavatory, Antique faucet trim, and assorted countertop accessories.

Prairie Flowers™ artist edition design is applied to a Floor Container, Anatole Pedestal Lavatory, and matching tiles.

A Marble Console Tabletop with Uccello legs in Weathered Black, Caxton under-counter lavatory in Tender Grey, and Antique faucet.

Queen Anne Double Basin Vanity hand crafted by Baker Furniture, with custom marble top and Prairie Flowers under-counter lavatories with matching trim on Antique faucets.

Queen Anne Single Basin Vanity with Caxton under-counter lavatory and Antique faucet.

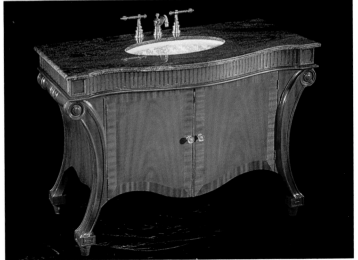

Stately Homes® Vanity with custom stone top, IV Georges Brass faucet, and Vintage under-counter lavatory with Classic Oak design.

# A Gallery of Great Designs

The following photos are a sampling of the great designs created for Kohler over the past two decades.

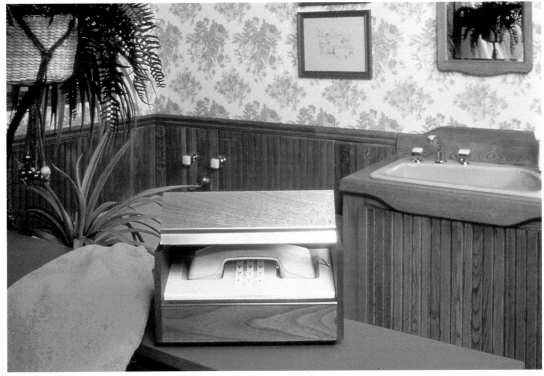

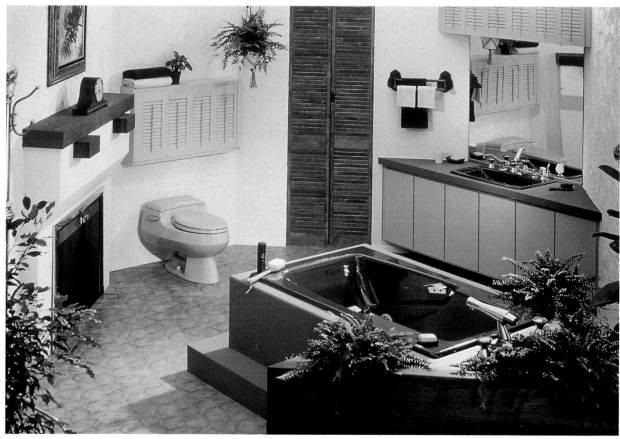

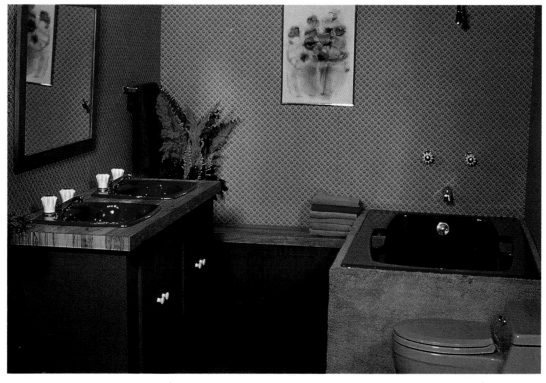

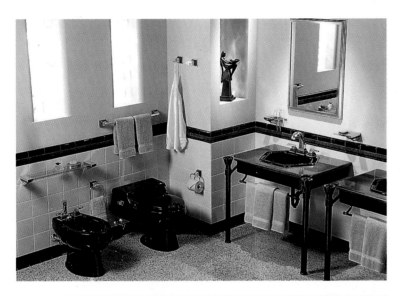

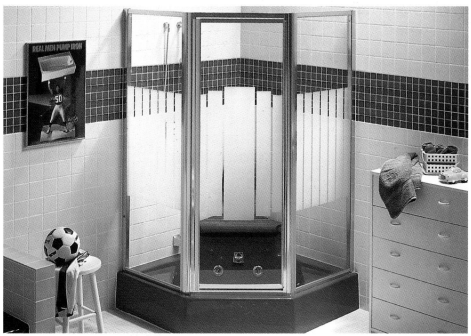

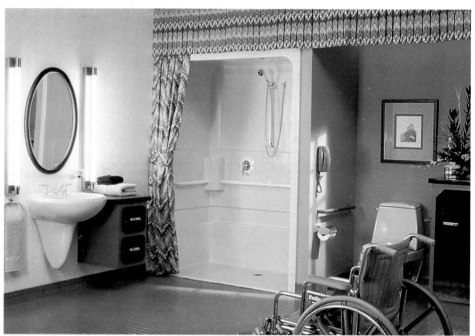